FAMILY connection

In-depth Bible Study

Discipline:
A Scriptural Foundation for Parenting

LEADER

by Ray Bardill and Roger Sonnenberg

CPH
SAINT LOUIS

Edited by Thomas J. Doyle

Write to the Library for the Blind, 1333 S. Kirkwood Road, St. Louis, MO 63122-7295, to obtain these materials in braille or in large type for the visually impaired.

Cover artwork: Michael Fleishmann

CONTENTS

Introduction

In-depth Study

This course follows what has come to be called an "in-depth" model of Bible study. The format was first introduced in CPH materials with the Life-Light series. In this context "in-depth study" includes these four components: individual daily home study; discussion in a small group; a lecture presentation; and a review (through reading a review leaflet) of the week's study.

Participants

Daily reading and study will require from 20 to 35 minutes for the five days preceding the group assembly. The day following the assembly will be spent reviewing the previous week's study by going over the completed study leaflet and reading the review leaflet.

Leaders

While the in-depth model this course proposes and begins with individual study and cannot achieve its aims without it, it cannot be completed by individual study alone. Trained leaders are necessary. These leaders include the following individuals, who perform the tasks listed here:

The Director

This person oversees the program in a local center (congregation or group of neighboring congregations). The director

- serves as the overall coordinator and leader;

- coordinates scheduling;

- orders materials;

- convenes leadership team meetings;

- develops publicity;

- recruits participants;

- maintains records and budgeting;

- assigns, with the leadership team, participants to small discussion groups;

- makes arrangements for facilities;

- communicates outreach opportunities to small-group leaders and to congregational boards;

- follows up on participants who leave the program.

The Presenter

This person prepares and delivers the lecture at the weekly assembly. The presenter also

- prepares worship material (devotional thought, hymn, prayer), using resources in the study leaflet and leaders guide and materials of the presenter's own choosing;

- helps the small-group discussion leaders grow in understanding the content of the lessons;

- encourages prayer at weekly leadership team meetings.

The Small-Group Coordinator

This person supervises and coordinates the work of the small-group discussion leaders. The small-group coordinator

- recruits, with the leadership team, the small-group discussion leaders;

- assists the director in follow-up of outreach through discussion leaders;

- encourages discussion leaders to contact absent group members;

- participates in weekly leadership-team and discussion-leaders equipping meetings.

The Small-Group Discussion Leaders

These people guide and facilitate discussion of participants in small groups. There should be one leader for each 10–12 participants. In no case should a small group include more than 12 members.

The small-group discussion leaders are, perhaps, those individuals who are most important to the success of the program. They should, therefore, be chosen with special care and equipped with the skills they will need to guide discussion and to foster a caring fellowship within the group. These discussion leaders

- prepare weekly for the small-group discussion by working through the study leaflet and leaders guide section for each session;

- encourage and assist their small group in prayer;

- foster fellowship and mutual care within the discussion group;

- attend weekly discussion-leaders training meetings.

The Weekly Schedule
Here's how the course will work week by week:

1. Each participant will receive a study leaflet at the beginning of each week of study. The study leaflet contains a hymn, a prayer, and other worship resources. These resources may be used in individual daily study and at the opening of the following week's assembly. The leaflet also contains readings and study questions for five days.

2. After the five days of home study, participants will gather for a weekly assembly of all participants. The assembly will begin with a brief period of worship (five minutes). Participants will then join their assigned discussion groups (of 12 or fewer), where they will go over the week's study questions together (55 minutes). These discussion groups will remain the same throughout the course.

Assembling together once again, participants will listen to a lecture on the concept they have studied the previous week and discussed in their small groups (20 minutes). After the lecture, the director or another leader will distribute the review leaflet for the previous session and the study leaflet for the coming week. Closing announcements and other necessary business may take another five minutes.

3. On the day following the assembly, participants will review the preceding week's work. They will review the study leaflet they completed (and which they may have supplemented or corrected during the discussion in their small group), and they will read the review leaflet, which recaps the lecture they heard.

Then the weekly study process begins all over again!

Acknowledgment

Discipline: A Scriptural Foundation for Parenting resulted from the initiative of the Lutheran Family Association (LFA), that proposed a series of family life courses in the LifeLight format. LFA desires to provide resources that will help parents and marriage partners apply biblical principles to their relationships and interactions. These resources are intended to be useful to Christians, as they draw their teaching directly and purely from the Bible for application to daily life.

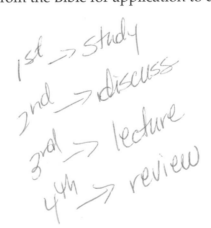

1st → study
2nd → discuss
3rd → lecture
4th → review

Opening Worship

Open the session by singing the hymn and reading the prayer in the study leaflet.

Hymn (see following page)

Day 1—God's Family as an Organization

1. a. In verse 12, both unity and diversity are expressed in the words, "a unit" and "many parts." Though God has given us different spiritual gifts, we are all members of the body of Christ. b. St. Paul dispels any spiritual pride in verses 21–26 by reminding us that every gift of every person is important just as every part of the human body is important and essential. "Its parts should have equal concern for each other" (v. 25b). c. Children are important. Scripture reminds us they are special gifts from God. St. Paul affirms the fact that even those who seem to have less important functions in the body of Christ are indispensable (1 Corinthians 12:22).

2. Allow participants to share how each member of their family is unique and irreplaceable.

3. If one person suffers in the family of God, all members suffer. If one member is honored, everyone is honored. A similar thought is expressed in the African proverb, "Even if he is your enemy, as long as he is of your tribe, it is bad to steal from him." In essence, we steal from ourselves when we steal from another since we are members of the same "tribe" or family.

4. It is easy to lose our own good common sense in dealing with our children, thus, it is important we meet with other people who can help us see things correctly and remind us of God's will.

Day 2—A Platform for God's Family

5. a. We are to "love the Lord [our] God with all [our] heart and with all [our] soul and with all [our] strength" (Deuteronomy 6:5). It is total love. b. In response to the Lord's total love for us without conditions, we love God and one another totally and without conditions. c. The results of God's love for His people is that His people respond in love to Him and to others. Jesus quoted Leviticus 19:18 against the Pharisees who thought it was legitimate to hate one's enemy.

6. When God's people forget the Lord God, they will perish and be destroyed like other nations who forgot before them (Deuteronomy 8:19–20).

7. a. Certainly many of the descriptions given in Romans 1:28–32 describe many communities today: "they invent ways of doing evil; they disobey their parents; they are senseless." b. The lack of discipline is really an indication of a broken relationship with God. St. Paul describes clearly in Romans 1 that when the vertical relationship with God is broken so the horizontal relationships with others also is damaged. There is a disregard and disrespect for others. We think more of ourselves than God or anyone else.

8. Allow for a time of reflection and prayer.

Day 3—God's Boundaries for His Family

9. Benjamin Franklin was right in saying that "we must all hang together, or most assuredly we shall … hang separately." Without boundaries there is chaos.

Children of the Heavenly Father

Text: Caroline V. Sandell Berg, 1832-1903; tr. Ernst W. Olson 1870-1958
    Copyright Board of Publications, Lutheran Church in America. Used by permission.
Tune: Swedish folk tune

TRYGGARE KAN INGEN VARA

L M

10. God loved His people so much that He established boundaries for them. He did this in the form of the Ten Commandments as recorded in Deuteronomy 5:1–22 and Exodus 20:2–17.

11. a. Christians have great advantages over non-Christians in the discipline they give to their children. For example, when they speak of forgiveness, they speak from the perspective of what God says. It's not pragmatic or relative. It doesn't change with time. It doesn't change with the circumstances. b. When Christian parents speak of the boundaries for their children, they have "a stable, fixed yardstick" for the establishment of these boundaries—God's Word. c. Two absolute boundaries must certainly include: "Love the Lord your God with all your heart and with all your soul and with all your mind" and "Love your neighbor as yourself" (Matthew 22:37, 39).

12. Allow for a time of personal prayer.

Day 4—His Promised Presence

13. a. Jesus wanted to clarify that His orders came from His heavenly Father when He said to His mother, "Dear woman, why do you involve me?" (John 2:4). He reminds her that His time had not yet come. b. Jesus' presence meant that the bridal couple would have sufficient wine for the wedding celebration. To be without wine would have been regarded as highly discourteous. c. Hopefully, the couple recognized the importance of having Jesus present at their marriage.

14. God assured His people of His presence through "a pillar of cloud to guide them on their way and by night in a pillar of fire to give them light, so that they could travel by day or night" (Exodus 13:21). These symbols were their constant guide.

15. God is with us always. It is a theme we heard when Jesus came in the flesh and was called "Immanuel"—meaning "God with us" (Matthew 1:23).

16. Encourage participants to invite Jesus to "be their guest" throughout the week.

Day 5—The Destructive Nature of Sin

17. God "gave them over to a depraved mind, to do what ought not to be done. They have become filled with every kind of wickedness, evil, greed, and depravity. They [were] full of envy, murder, strife, deceit and malice … gossips, slanderers, God-haters, insolent, arrogant and boastful … they invent ways of doing evil … disobey their parents … are senseless, faithless, heartless, ruthless …" (Romans 1:28–31). They know what God wants them to do, and they not only disobey His commands but they applaud others who do.

18. a. Parents falsely assume their children are "little adults," thus expecting them to act in a certain way. When children are born they are not rational and well-behaved. Adults should not expect them to act like "little adults." b. Children are born sinful and selfish. They want what they want from the time they are born with little consideration for anyone but themselves. c. Remember, children are not "little adults," and so they do not reason logically, and as reasonable as your discipline might be, they may not comprehend and understand.

19. Husbands and wives have unrealistic expectations of each other. Parents and children have unrealistic expectations of one another. We need to remember, if any of us were perfect, there would never have been a need for a Savior.

20. St. Paul reminds us that "through the obedience of the one man [Jesus] the many will be made righteous" (Romans 5:19). This includes every family member, young and old.

21. Allow for a time of personal prayer.

Lecture—Session 1

It Takes a Village to Raise a Child

A mother and her two-year-old son moved to a small community in Kansas. One night the little boy left the backyard of their home and got lost in a thousand-acre field of wheat directly behind the house. When the mother reported him missing, the sheriff organized a large group of people to search the surrounding areas. They searched throughout the night but to no avail. The child could not be found. The night time temperature dropped well below freezing.

Just as they were ready to give up the next morning, a group of men decided to join hands and make a wide sweep across the field. They had joined hands and in a short while they stumbled across the child. The child had obviously fallen and had been hurt. Unable to walk he remained huddled in the wheat throughout the night and had died of exposure.

As they placed the young child's body into the arms of the young mother, she cried out, "Why didn't you join hands sooner? Why didn't you join hands sooner?"

Why didn't you join hands sooner?

The truth is God created families to be in relationship with one another, to join hands and be His "workmanship … to do good works, which God prepared in advance for us to do" (Ephesians 2:10). Within the family there is both unity and diversity in order for the work to be done well. Everyone is important. Children. Parents. Grandparents.

One of the important tasks for every parent is to *deparent*, "to train one's children with ample life skills so that the children, might be set free to live God-pleasing, responsible lives, without depending on their parents." (Carl Sparkman, *Parents Passing on the Faith*, Victor Books, Wheaton, IL, 1989.) A part of such deparenting includes discipline. It means saying "no" at times; at other times it means saying, "You've done a great job!" It is joining hands with God Himself in raising His children so that they might bring Him glory and honor.

train to set free to live as God commanded

By now we've all heard the African proverb, "It takes a village to raise a child." A book by the same title received notoriety in one of the recent presidential campaigns. Some felt that the book suggested too strong a governmental role in the raising of children. Whatever our opinion, however, the truth of the matter is, raising a child takes a consortium of people. It especially takes a mother and father who love their children enough to discipline them.

It Takes a Family with a Platform to Raise a Child

Every political party during a presidential election adopts a certain platform. The platform contains the major tenets of the party and the political stance to which the presidential candidate vows his allegiance. When God called His people out of Egypt and into a new, promised land, He gave them a platform. Moses instructed God's people in these commandments and asked them in turn to teach these commandments to their children. With the platform came a promise. If they obeyed and kept His decrees they would "enjoy long life" (Deuteronomy 6:2).

The platform contained words which eventually became known as the Shema, or the Jewish confession of faith. This confession was so important to them that they would repeat it daily. It consisted of: "Hear, O Israel: The LORD our God, the LORD is one. Love the LORD your God with all your heart and with all your soul and with all your strength" (Deuteronomy 6:4–5). Even today pious Jews recite this creed twice daily.

To "love the Lord your God with all your heart and with all your soul and with all your strength" is a basic platform tenet not only for the Jews but it is essential for every family today as well. Families who forget God become futile in their thinking and their hearts are darkened (Romans 1:21). The consequences of forgetting God are evident in many families today and are described clearly in Romans 1:28–31:

> Furthermore, since they did not think it worthwhile to retain the knowledge of God, He gave them over to a depraved mind, to do what ought not to be done. They have become filled with every kind of wickedness, evil, greed and depravity. They are full of envy, murder, strife, deceit and malice. They are gossips, slanderers, God-haters, insolent, arrogant and boastful; they invent ways of doing evil; they disobey their

Notes:

parents; they are senseless, faithless, heartless, ruthless. Although they know God's righteous decree that those who do such things deserve death, they do not only continue to do these very things but also approve of those who practice them.

In a day and age when so many politicians and educators, counselors and parents, are asking "What's happened to the American family?" perhaps, it is time we go back to the basic tenet set forth by God early in the history of the Israelites— to "love the LORD … with all your heart." Perhaps it is time for us to ask whether or not we are impressing this truth on our children's hearts. Are we talking with our children about their relationship with God? Are we writing "them on the doorframes of [our] houses"? (Deuteronomy 6:7–9). Do our children know that it is our highest daily goal personally to love God with all our heart and soul? If so, how do they know it? What evidence do they have to know that our house serves the Lord?

It Takes a Family with Boundaries to Raise a Child

Many children today cry out for discipline. They cry out, "Give me rules!" They cry out, "Love me enough to punish me when I break these rules."

The Bible shows us how our heavenly Father cares for us. He cared enough to establish boundaries for us. He did this in the form of the Ten Commandments as recorded in Deuteronomy 5:1–22 and Exodus 20:2–17. These laws have formed the basis for most of Western civilization's thinking on right and wrong. They were not only binding upon the Jews but binding also for all believers.

God set Boundries 10 - commandments

Remember Christ's conversation with the young ruler about keeping the commandments if he desired to "enter life" (Matthew 19:17)? Though they are most certainly binding on each and everyone of us, it is only through grace that man is righteous before God. To the rich young ruler who thought he had kept the commandments, Jesus was saying, "But you haven't, no matter what you think, no one can keep the Law perfectly … so you need a Savior."

Jesus Christ came, because as hard as each of us have tried, we've crossed the boundaries. We cannot keep on the pathway set before us by God. But thanks be to God there is forgiveness through Jesus Christ. He puts us back on the path once again. Nothing is more important than to know His forgiveness and to experience it daily in our homes.

It Takes a Family with God's Presence to Raise a Child

God's presence in a family always makes a difference, just as it made a difference at the wedding of Cana. Throughout John's gospel different miracles are described as "signs" (John 2:11). These miracles displayed Jesus' glory as predicted in the Old Testament: "The desert and the parched land will be glad; the wilderness will rejoice and blossom. Like the crocus, it will burst into bloom; it will rejoice greatly and shout for joy. The glory of Lebanon will be given to it, the splendor of Carmel and Sharon; they will see the glory of the LORD, the splendor of our God" (Isaiah 35:1–2).

In the case of the wedding feast at Cana, Jesus turned water into wine. To run out of wine was regarded as an act of discourtesy for a host. But Jesus had been invited as a guest. Jesus' presence meant help was available!

Through Word and Sacrament, Jesus continues to come to us over and over again. He speaks to us and abides in us. His presence means miracles. It means special power for each and every one of us, power to be families who serve Him and Him alone. St. Paul prays,

> I pray … that the eye of your heart may be enlightened in order that you may know … His incomparably great power for us who believe. That power is like the working of His mighty strength, which He exerted in Christ when He raised Him from the dead and seated Him at His right hand in the heavenly realms (Ephesians 1:18–20).

As parents we need to ask, "Does our discipline reflect God's presence?" "Are our words loving?" "Our actions?" Our prayer must be, "Come Lord Jesus, be our guest in our homes. Be present in the way we talk, in the way we act, in the way we discipline."

> Abide with us, our Savior,
> Nor let Your mercy cease;
> From Satan's might defend us,
> And give our hearts Your peace.

Notes:

w/ Jesus we have help

C

Abide with us, our Helper,
Sustain us by Your Word;
Let us and all Your people
To living faith be stirred.

Abide with us, Redeemer,
O Light, eternal Light;
Your truth direct and guide us
To flee from error's night.

Abide in princely bounty
With us, large-hearted Lord,
Our lives with grace and wisdom
Enriching through Your Word.

It Takes a Family with Realistic Expectations

A family of God knows that there is no perfection to be found here on earth, especially in their family. They not only don't expect it, they don't demand it. This doesn't mean that children can do whatever … whenever. It doesn't mean that sin is tolerated. It isn't. It means that they know perfection belongs alone to the Lord Jesus Christ. Families celebrate perfection but always in light of the righteousness given to them as a gift from Jesus Christ: "Consequently, just as the result of one trespass was condemnation for all men, so also the result of one act of righteousness was justification that brings life for all men" (Romans 5:18).

In all our parenting, we need to ask, "Are our expectations for our children too high?" "Are we expecting perfection from them when we don't expect it of ourselves?" "Do we expect them to act like little adults when they're not adults?"

Yes, it takes a family to raise a child, a family …

- with a platform tenet that says, "Love the LORD your God with all your heart and with all your soul and with all your strength" (Deuteronomy 6:5);

- with boundaries, beginning with the Ten Commandments;

- with God's presence, assuring us of love and power; and

- with realistic expectations, knowing perfection belongs alone to the Lord Jesus Christ.

Notes:

Opening Worship

Open the session by singing the hymn and reading the prayer in the study leaflet.

Hymn (see following page)

Day 1—Belonging

1. a. Though the giant stood before him, David knew "the Lord who delivered [him] from the paw of the lion and the paw of the bear [would] deliver [him] from the hand of this Philistine" (v. 37). b. Though David's argument was good, it would have been difficult for most commanders to let someone of such size and inexperience to go out and fight the giant. c. The Philistines are scorning Yahweh, the God of Israel. David emphasizes that he is acting as champion for God, not so much for Israel. The Philistines were defying "the living God" Himself. It was for God's honor and His name that David wanted to face the giant.

2. a. As a faithful shepherd himself, David knew a good shepherd would always take care of his sheep. He would make them "lie down in green pastures" (v. 2). b. David was anointed in the Lord by Samuel. In the anointing, "the Spirit of the Lord came upon [him] in power" (1 Samuel 16:13). He was empowered by God Himself.

3. a. David could face the enemy, confident that his strength came from God. b. David's peace of mind came from the fact that he knew he was a child of God, and his heavenly Father would never forsake him. c. David knew that God was guiding him along the correct path for his life.

4. Children misbehave in different ways in an attempt to feel they belong. They may act obnoxious or throw a tantrum in an attempt to be noticed and feel they belong. It is known that many teenagers join gangs in order to fulfill this basic need of belonging. They will join even the wrong people if it means becoming a part of a group or a "family."

5. Have the group brainstorm on ways to assure their children they are important parts of their family, and the family of God.

Day 2—"Just Pay Attention to Me"

6. a. The children of Israel rebelled simply because of their sinful hearts. What we see happening here is open apostasy. They had just entered into a covenant with God. They had heard the law and had pledged themselves to obey it. When Moses had failed to reappear they believed God had abandoned them. b. Moses had only been on the mountain 40 days and 40 nights (Exodus 24:18). c. Aaron "built an altar in front of the calf" and said there was going to be a festival of celebration. They practiced gross idolatry. d. Parents so often use the easiest and fastest way to handle a discipline problem instead of taking time to do something that would be more effective and long-term. For example, some parents simply turn on the television as a way of babysitting their children, keeping them quiet and out of their way. They might simply give them what they want as opposed to taking the time to explain why it isn't the best thing for them right now. e. Aaron blames the people instead of taking any responsibility himself, similar to what Adam and Eve did after they had sinned. Each blamed the other for their sin (Genesis 3:12–13). f. Surely one of the most common concerns today among many people is the lack of discipline and disrespect children show toward other adults, especially their parents. The Israelites were "out of control and so [were] a laughingstock to their enemies" (Exodus 32:25). We also become a laughingstock to our enemies when we let our children run wild without any restraints.

7. Children will do whatever gets them attention, even if it means misbehaving.

8. Lead the group in a prayer asking God to help them ignore their children's misbehavior and give attention during good behavior.

Chief of Sinners Though I Be

1 Chief of sinners though I be, Jesus shed his
2 Oh, the height of Jesus' love, High - er than the
3 On - ly Jesus can im-part Balm to heal the
4 Chief of sinners though I be, Christ is all in
5 O my Sav - ior, help af - ford By your Spir - it

blood for me, Died that I might live on high,
heav'ns a - bove, Deep - er than the depths of sea,
wound - ed heart, Peace that flows from sin for - giv'n,
all to me; All my wants to him are known,
and your Word! When my way - ward heart would stray,

Lives that I might nev - er die. As the branch is
Last - ing as e - ter - ni - ty! Love that found me—
Joy that lifts the soul to heav'n, Faith and hope to
All my sor - rows are his own. He sus - tains the
Keep me in the nar - row way; Grace in time of

to the vine, I am his, and he is mine.
won - drous thought— Found me when I sought him not.
walk with God In the way that E - noch trod.
hid - den life Safe with him from earth - ly strife.
need sup - ply While I live and when I die.

Text: William McComb, 1793-1873
Tune: Richard Redhead, 1820-1901

GETHSEMANE
7 7 7 7 7 7

Day 3—"Who's in Control Here?"

Children are no different than adults. They want power. They want to know that they're impacting what surrounds them even if it is through misbehavior.

9. a. Herod was most disturbed that another ruler was coming out of Bethlehem, one who would "be the shepherd of … Israel" (Matthew 2:6). b. Herod obviously thought he could outwit God, that God was not almighty or omnipotent. c. Herod was willing to "kill all the boys in Bethlehem and its vicinity who were two years old and under" (Matthew 2:16). He was desperate. He would do whatever he could humanly do to get rid of a potential new ruler.

10. Some ways that parents misuse their power is through bribery ("If you do your chores, I'll give you some ice cream.") or guilt trips ("You must not love me because you never clean your room!").

11. By your getting highly emotional the child recognizes that he/she has made an impact on the world around him, even if it's a negative impact. Children see they have power when they get you upset.

12. Allow for a time of personal reflection and prayer.

Day 4—"I'll Get Even!"

13. a. God does not need trickery or scheming to achieve His purposes. It was God's plan to have Jacob receive the birthright but He in no way approved of what Rebekah and Jacob did to try to accomplish that goal. b. Countless children today are crying out "Bless me—me too, my father!" (v. 34). They may be crying out for approval or acceptance. Perhaps it is a son crying out for his father's affirmation. It might be a daughter who has always had to compete against an older sister. She's not as gifted intellectually but more athletic. Her parents keep bringing up her sister's achievements without recognizing hers. c. Remember, Esau had previously sold his birthright to Jacob for a bowl of "red stew" (Genesis 25:30). Though he had given away his birthright he quickly forgot or ignored what he had done and started to prepare to receive it from his father (Genesis 27:2–4). d. Rebekah continued to deceive her family even after it was discovered that the birthright had been given to Jacob instead of Esau. Because Esau sought revenge against his broth-

er, Rebekah convinced both Jacob and Isaac that he must leave town for a while. She convinced her husband Isaac it was because Jacob might marry a Canaanite woman if he didn't (Genesis 27:46).

14. Neither Rebekah nor Jacob took responsibility for the wrong they had perpetrated. Jacob went off without ever confessing his sin. Rebekah never told her own husband she had sinned and needed his forgiveness.

15. Jacob may have inwardly wanted his father's acceptance especially since we read that Isaac loved Esau more than Jacob.

16. There are many things parents can do to make a child feel like he/she belongs and has significance. If the child is revengeful, you yourself might need to withdraw for a moment or two to avoid retaliating yourself. It should be your goal to win cooperation and supply encouragement to the child, letting him/her know that he/she does belong and does have significance. This sometimes needs to be very intentional.

Day 5—"What's the Use?"

There are some children who feel so inadequate that they simply give up and hope others will leave them alone.

17. a. Adam's excuse that he hid himself "because he was naked" was only half true because his feeling of nakedness came about as a consequence of his disobedience. He and his wife were hiding because they had sinned, they had blatantly disobeyed God. They tried to find refuge from God in the very sanctuary of God. b. Some people feel God could not possibly like them because of their sin. They say things like, "The church will fall in if I ever show up" or "When I straighten out my life I'll be back to church." This feeling of inadequacy is carried into relationships with other people as well. There are many people who feel they don't really matter, they have no significance and thus hide from having contact with other people.

18. The chief priests might have listened to Judas, spent some time with him, talking to him about how he was feeling. It was evident, however, that the chief priests had no remorse and little sensitivity for anyone other than themselves.

19. We are called God's "chosen people." We belong to God Himself, to His family, because of Jesus Christ. He declared us holy through His life, death, and resurrection. There are many Scriptural verses which remind us of our importance in Christ: 1 Corinthians 6:19–20; Ephesians 1:3–10; 1 John 3:1 just to name a few.

20. Allow for a time of discussion and personal prayer.

Lecture—Session 2

Goals of Behavior

Could it be?

We're so busy giving our kids what we didn't have that we don't take time to give them what we do have.

Could it be?

It's not how many fish you caught with your son, it's how many times you went fishing with him.

Could it be?

A child is not as he sees himself.
He is not as you see him either.
He is as he sees himself in your eyes.

There are many things a parent can give a child; however there are few things more important than a sense of belonging. Children and adults need to know that they are significant, that they belong. Research has shown that children will go to great extremes to belong; even join gangs or religious cults.

David and His Sense of Belonging

Scripture paints pictures of people who knew they belonged—belonged to a sovereign God who loved them and cared for them. The story of David comes to mind as he faced the giant Goliath. The Philistine army had challenged the armies of Saul. In those days it was common to try to win the battle through intimidation. The Philistines paraded their hero before the Israelites, the world heavyweight champion—Goliath. *The Guinness Book of World Records* reports that Robert Pershing Wadlow, the tallest man who ever lived, measured 8 feet 11 inches. Goliath's height was about 10 feet. His armor was as impressive as his size: "He had a bronze helmet on his head and wore a coat of scale armor of bronze weighing five thousand shekels; on his legs he wore bronze greaves, and a bronze javelin was slung on his back. His spear shaft was like a weaver's rod, and its iron point weighed six hundred shekels" (1 Samuel 17:5–7a).

Everyone shies away from Goliath's challenge, including Saul. Only one feels confident enough to meet the challenge—David. It is not that he's so big, he isn't. He simply knows who he is and to whom he belongs—God. He is willing to fight, not for the sake of the Israelites, but for the sake of God, His Creator! "The LORD who delivered me from the paw of the lion and the paw of the bear will deliver me from the hand of this Philistine" (1 Samuel 17:37).

Knowing that He belonged to God was key not only to David's willingness to meet Goliath face-to-face but also to his victory. "You come against me with sword and spear and javelin, but I come against you in the name of the LORD Almighty, the God of the armies of Israel, whom you have defied" (1 Samuel 17:45). Victory was his; "Reaching into his bag and taking out a stone, he slung it and struck the Philistine on the forehead. The stone sank into his forehead,… and he fell facedown on the ground" (1 Samuel 17:49). David reiterated confidence in God time and time again in his psalms: "Those who know Your name will trust in You, for You, LORD, have never forsaken those who seek You" (Psalm 9:10); "Even though I walk through the valley of the shadow of death, I will fear no evil, for You are with me" (Psalm 23:4a).

Christians need to let their children know they belong because they do truly belong. They belong to God Himself through the blood of Jesus Christ. They belong to God through the very life, death, and resurrection of Jesus Christ. Through Him they are brought into relationship with God and with one another. Through their Baptism they are united with Him; we are united with "Him … in His death … [and] with Him in His resurrection" (Romans 6:5). Peter further clarified what this meant when he wrote: "But you are a chosen people, a royal priesthood, a holy nation, a people belonging to God, that you may declare the praise of Him who called you out of darkness into His wonderful light. Once you were not a people, but now you are the people of God; once you had not received mercy, but now you have received mercy" (1 Peter 2:9–10).

Christianity is about relationships, not individualism. It is about people belonging to God and to one another! It is about worth, so much worth that God Himself would send His only-begotten Son, not "to condemn the world, but to save the world through Him" (John 3:16–17).

Children will often misbehave if they do not feel they belong or are appreciated. The misbehavior may be seen in a number of ways. It may be demonstrated in throwing a temper tantrum or being outright obnoxious. Our reaction might simply be, "You have an attitude. Go to your room until you can change."

Rudolph Dreikers, a well-known child psychologist, claimed that children (and adults) behave in certain ways in order to know they belong and have significance. Sometimes they may think the way they belong is if they have a parent's undivided attention, even if through misbehavior. The child may know that he should do his homework before he goes to bed, but he knows if he doesn't do it, he'll get his mother's attention!

God's people often demonstrate such an attitude. Repeatedly they seem to say, "Pay attention to us or otherwise we'll misbehave." Thinking Moses was spending too much time up on the mountain away from them, the children of Israel misbehaved. They ate and drank "and got up to indulge in revelry" around a golden calf, an idol formed from their jewelry (Exodus 32:6). Throughout their history, the Israelites were known to do everything from pout to scold God for the things that were happening in their lives. "Was it because there were no graves in Egypt that You brought us to the desert to die? What have You done to us by bringing us out of Egypt?" (Exodus 14:11–12).

Instead of forcing our children to seek attention through misbehavior it can be our goal to give them attention during pleasant times, thus reinforcing suitable and more pleasant behavior. In order to do this we might intentionally set special times with our child on a regular basis in order to give him/her special attention. One father intentionally sets aside one day every two to three months to be with one of his children. For his children "love" is spelled: "T I M E."

Another way children feel they belong is when they have power, when they can control a situation. Children can easily control a given situation, even if the power comes through misbehavior.

When they realize they have the power to make an impact on the situation, a sense of belonging is realized. Think of a child throwing rocks into a calm lake. It might be to see how far he can throw the rocks. It might be to simply watch the effect or the impact he has on the water after the initial splash of the rock. Ripples fan out from the initial impact. He notes he has had an impact, an effect on the water.

A child may see that he has impact on the world around him by making her/his parents angry. Even though the child may not like his/her misbehavior, at the same time she/he feels good that, as small as she/he may be, she/he can cause "ripples."

Parents should not allow their emotions to get the best of them during the times when their children are mis-behaving. When they misbehave and we do get upset, children see they have caused some "ripples." They have had an impact on the world around them. When you react emotionally, you reinforce their negative behavior. In order not to react emotionally, we may have to simply take time to cool off. Often such restraint comes only through the help that God gives through Word and Sacrament and prayers.

Jack and Judith Balswick in their book, *The Family*, differentiate between "power" and "empowerment." Too often people seek to have power, to control. God's way is not to control another but to "empower" another. To empower another means to make the other person everything he or she can be. It "is the process of instilling confidence, of strengthening and building children up to become more powerful and competent." He makes it clear that "the most effective empowerers are those individuals who have them-selves been empowered by the unconditional love of God and the Holy Spirit. (*The Family*, by Jack Balswick and Judith Balswick, Baker Book House, Grand Rapids, Mich., 1991.)

Parents need to ask themselves: What are we showing our children when we control with power? In what ways can we "empower" instead of "control"? How can we make our children everything God wants them to be?

Revenge and Feeling Inadequate

Children will misbehave at times simply to get even. If they've been hurt they want to hurt in return. Such was the case of the man who wrote:

> I'm disgusted with my brother;
> I am positively sore,
> I have never been so angry
> With a human being before.

He's everything detestable
That's spelled with A through Z,
He deserves to be the target
Of a ten-pound bumble bee.

I'd like to wave a magic wand
And make him disappear,
Or watch a wild rhinoceros
Attack him from the rear.

Perhaps I'll cook a pot of soup
And dump my brother in;
He forgot today's my birthday!
Oh, how could he … he's my twin.

(*Sharpening the Sword,* by Stephen D. Hower, CPH, 1996.

Children are no different than many adults. They say to themselves, "You hurt me, I'll hurt you in return!!!" When they "get back," at least they'll have shown him/her what it feels like to not belong, to not be significant!

Throughout Scripture there are examples of people who sought revenge. When Esau failed to receive the blessing of his father, he sought Jacob's life. "Esau held a grudge against Jacob because of the blessing his father had given him. He said to himself, 'The days of mourning for my father are near; then I will kill my brother Jacob' " (Genesis 27:41). Though revenge may give a momentary satisfaction to the one taking it, it can destroy that person; setting up destructive life patterns which can eventually lead even to spiritual destruction.

When Esau cried out to his father, "Bless me—me too, my father!" he was crying out as many children cry out today with their misbehavior:

"Dad, show me you care, care even enough to say 'no!' " "Show me that you love me as much as you love my sister." Preventing a pattern of revenge means setting up a schedule for spending time with the child on a regular basis. It means encouraging the child. It means letting the child know he belongs!

When a child feels like he does not belong and nothing he does will make him belong, he may simply give up. Rod was 17 years old. For years he never felt wanted by his step-father and mother. He wanted to know that they cared and did everything from

Notes:

highjacking a car to skipping school to learn if they did. His suicide note read, "… Dad doesn't care. My stepdad hates, as he said, 'to look at my ugly face.' You, mom, are too busy with your new baby to care about me. And so, I'm out of here …." He wanted to belong, but everyone, including his own mom, didn't seem to care.

Every child, every adult, needs to know that someone cares for them. As Christians we can tell one another God cares; "How great is the love the Father has lavished on us, that we should be called children of God! And that is what we are!" (1 John 3:1). Because He loves us so, we can love one another. We can "be kind and compassionate to one another, forgiving each other, just as in Christ God [forgives us]" (Ephesians 4:32). We can say and show our children and our children's children that they belong to God the Father, and God the Son, and God the Holy Spirit, forever and ever. Amen.

Notes:

Opening Worship

Open the session by singing the hymn and reading the prayer in the study leaflet.

Hymn (see following page)

Day 1—Love Gives Birth to Love

1. Normally, someone who says, "I love you," means that he/she values the person, he/she gets a lot of pleasure from being around him/her, etc.

2. a. Hardship indicates a deep love between a parent and his/her child. It indicates a true parent-child relationship; "Endure hardship as discipline; God is treating you as sons. For what son is not disciplined by his father? If you are not disciplined (and everyone undergoes discipline), then you are illegitimate children and not true sons" (Hebrews 12:7–8). b. Our heavenly Father and our earthly fathers love us too much not to discipline us, or educate us. An undisciplined child will only know unhappiness through life. c. God's discipline differs from our earthly father's discipline in that "our fathers disciplined us for a little while as they thought best; but God disciplines us for our good, that we may share in His holiness" (Hebrews 12:10).

3. a. False. Man is not intrinsically loving. By nature he is evil and "dead in [his] transgressions and sins" (Ephesians 2:1). b. True. "We love because He first loved us" (1 John 4:19). In loving us, God not only shows us what real love is but He also empowers us with that love to love our children. c. True. Love knows no limits as was demonstrated in Jesus Christ laying down His life for us.

4. Though there are many things a parent can do to teach their children to be loving toward others, it always begins by teaching them about God's love. Loving is something that is best taught by example. A child will love as she/he has been

loved. A parent also can reinforce loving behavior through encouragement and affirmation when good behavior occurs.

5. Allow for a time of silent reflection.

Day 2—Kindness Gives Birth to Kindness

6. a. Jesus asks Peter three times whether or not he loves Him (John 21:15–17). b. To "truly love" or to love another with one's entire personality means that one loves with his whole being. He demonstrates it with actions, emotions, and words. c. The threefold challenge to Peter by Jesus—"Do you love Me?"—is closely parallel to his threefold denial (John 18:15–18, 25–27). Just as he denied Jesus three times, now Peter was given the opportunity to confess his love for Him three times. d. Just as Jesus never stopped loving Peter even though he had been disobedient, a loving parent never stops loving his/her child even though the child is disobedient. The parent reprimands but loves at the same time.

7. The qualities listed in Ephesians 4:31–32 are bitterness, rage and anger, brawling and slander, malice, kindness, compassion, and forgiveness. Forgiveness gives birth to forgiveness. Kindness gives birth to kindness. Compassion gives birth to compassion.

8. a. False. Kindness is not tolerating wrongdoing or evil. To tolerate evil is itself evil. b. False. Kindness is not leniency; in fact, it is the opposite. To allow a child to misbehave is being unkind, because an undisciplined child will eventually experience unhappiness. c. True. Kindness is not easy. It takes time. It is intentional. It requires work. d. True. Kindness needs to be forceful and persistent so the child has no doubts about his/her boundaries. It must be persistent because

Blest Be the Tie That Binds

1 Blest be the tie that binds Our hearts in Chris - tian love;
2 Be - fore our Fa - ther's throne We pour our ar - dent prayers;
3 We share our mu - tual woes, Our mu - tual bur - dens bear,
4 From sor - row, toil, and pain And sin we shall be free,

The u - ni - ty of heart and mind Is like to that a - bove.
Our fears, ours hopes, our aims are one, Our com - forts and our cares.
And of - ten for each oth - er flows The sym - pa - thiz - ing tear.
And per - fect love and friend - ship reign Through all e - ter - ni - ty.

Text: John Fawcett, 1740-1817, alt.
Tune: Lowell Mason, 1792-1872

BOYLSTON
S M

otherwise a child will be unclear and confused as to what he/she should do.

9. Lead the group in praying Ephesians 4:31–32.

Day 3—Consistency Builds Consistency

10. a. The psalmist considers the following three aspects of God's divine nature: (1) His greatness (v. 3); (2) His graciousness and mercy (v. 8); (3) His justice or righteousness (v. 17). b. God's consistent loving treatment of His children can be verified by "one generation" after another. "They will tell of Your mighty acts" (Psalm 145:4b). "The Lord is faithful to all His promises" (Psalm 145:13b). c. God's justice is consistent. He is "compassionate and gracious … slow to anger, abounding in love and faithfulness, maintaining love to thousands, and forgiving wickedness, rebellion and sin. Yet He does not leave the guilty unpunished; He punishes the children and their children for the sin of the fathers to the third and fourth generation" (Exodus 34:6b–7).

11. a. True. In Scripture we see how God parents His children and, thus, we are taught how to parent our own children. b. True. As a parent God is consistent. The rules that were true yesterday are true today. He doesn't change with the wind. Thus, God teaches us through His consistent parenting to parent our children with consistency. c. True. Rules and consequences should remain the same otherwise children wonder if the rules were really very important in the first place.

12. If moods determine a parent's rules and consequences of breaking the rules, children are taught that standards aren't really that important, at least not as important as the attitude one might have or a mood that one might be in.

13. Allow for a time of quiet reflection and prayer.

Day 4—Respect Gives Birth to Respect

14. To respect someone says "you're valuable." When you respect someone you're saying that a person's thoughts and feelings are important. They count.

15. a. Jesus showed great respect for both Simon the Pharisee and the woman. Even though the Pharisee's intent in inviting Jesus to his house may have been to entrap Him, Jesus, nevertheless, used the time wisely to teach a valuable lesson on the importance of people in the eyes of God. The woman was known to live a "sinful life," yet Jesus did not show disrespect to her. He gladly received her gesture of love as she kissed His feet and poured perfume on them. b. Jesus tells the story about the two men to explain to Simon why this woman was so extravagant in her love for Him. She had sinned greatly. The greater her sin the greater her love for Him because the more she was forgiven by Him. c. The woman's faith was great. She recognized she had been forgiven. She could leave the house filled with peace. Forgiveness always brings peace to a person.

16. The world says, "You must earn respect or deserve it." God says people are to be respected even if they don't earn it or deserve it. This does not mean tolerating wrongdoing, but it does mean one needs to "respect," meaning seeing the other person as God would see him/her.

17. a–c. Open a discussion of the different love languages. Allow participants to share what they believe to be their children's primary love language and what they can do to help fill their emotional "love tank." Pray, asking God to help each parent respect their child's style of loving.

Day 5—Patience Gives Birth to Patience

18. a. "The spirit is willing, but the body is weak" (Mark 14:38b). We know what the Lord wants us to do, but sometimes our emotions get the best of us and we act unbecoming of a Christian. b. Jesus demonstrated great patience with His disciples. Time and time again He returned only to find the disciples sleeping, failing to "watch and pray" with Him during this difficult time. Though He stated His disappointment, He nevertheless continued loving them. c. Be honest in assessing which areas of discipline you need God's help in. Correctly identifying the problem is already half the battle won.

19. God's Word describes patience as being a characteristic of love (1 Corinthians 13:4). In living "a life worthy of the calling you have received" one is to "be patient, bearing with one another in love" (Ephesians 4:1–2). St. Paul reminds the Thessalonian Christians they are to "be patient with everyone" (1 Thessalonians 5:14). They were to understand that no one is perfect. Everyone makes mistakes, is tempted, and has troubles. They were to be patient with each other as God is patient with us (2 Peter 3:9).

20. a. Give participants time for quiet meditation.
b. Read aloud Ephesians 4:32 and Galatians 5:22.
c. Lead the group in prayer, asking for patience.

Lecture—Session 3

Key Ingredients to Discipline

The story is told of the Pope who stood on the balcony in St. Peter's Square addressing his people. Thousands had gathered to hear him. Before he closed with a blessing of peace he said, "I have some bad news for you my children. The doctors tell me my heart has worn out and that I need a new one. Which one of you would be willing to give me your heart for such a transplant so that I might continue to serve God?"

Thousands waved their arms in the air shouting, "Me Papa, Me Papa."

The Pope was overwhelmed at the outpouring of love. "I am so moved by your generosity," he said, "In order to choose which one will give his heart to me, I will throw out a feather and the person on which it lands is the lucky person who will be given the privilege of giving me his heart."

He threw a feather from the balcony. It floated downward slowly but surely. However, it hovered in the air much longer than he expected, in fact, it did not seem to want to land. He hurried down from his balcony to the ground floor to see what was happening. As he stepped out into the crowd, he noticed to his surprise that all the people were blowing the feather away from them whenever it appeared as if it was going to land on them.

Sometimes, what we say and what we do are two different things! It's easy to talk. It's harder to walk the talk! And yet God says, "Dear children, let us not love with words or tongue but with actions and in truth" (1 John 3:18).

Walking the Talk of Love

There is no ingredient more important than the ingredient of love. St. Paul made it clear that one can have all the knowledge of good parenting, but if the knowledge is not disseminated with love, it is useless (1 Corinthians 13:2a). One can "have a faith that can move mountains, but have not love," it is then worth nothing (1 Corinthians 13:2b). He goes on to describe what love looks like: "Love is patient, love is kind. It does not envy, it does not boast, it is not proud. It is not rude, it is not self-seeking, it is not easily angered, it keeps no record of wrongs. Love does not delight in evil but rejoices with the truth. It always protects, always trusts, always hopes, always perseveres. Love never fails." (1 Corinthians 13:4–8).

Most parents love their children. The unfortunate thing is, no one can truly love their children as described by St. Paul unless they are connected to Jesus Christ—and then only imperfectly. It is only through the love that God pours into us by His grace that we are able to truly love, with kindness, patience, etc. "We love because He first loved us" (1 John 4:19).

A loving parent disciplines! The Greek word for discipline is *paideia*. It means "to educate."

"For what son is not disciplined by his father? If you are not disciplined [and everyone undergoes discipline], then you are illegitimate children and not true sons. Moreover, we have all had human fathers who disciplined us and we respected them for it. How much more should we submit to the Father of our spirits and live!" (Hebrews 12:7–9).

Discipline encourages, because it says we have someone who loves us enough to correct us, "to educate" us in the way that we should go.

Walking the talk of love means that we discipline in love. We not only say, "I'm doing this because I love you," but our actions themselves show them that we love. We not only speak the truth in love, we actually discipline in love. It would be helpful each time we discipline our child to ask ourselves, "Do our words and our actions show the child we love her/him?"

Walking the Talk of Kindness

When Jesus asked Peter three times if he loved Him, three times Peter replied, "You know that I love You" (John 21:15). The meaning of the word "love" as Peter used it was that he loved with his whole being. It means loving someone with more than words, but with acts of kindness.

Kindness is not something that comes naturally for a parent or for a child.

Notes:

"Those controlled by the sinful nature cannot please God. You, however, are controlled not by the sinful nature but by the Spirit, if the Spirit of God lives in you. And if anyone does not have the Spirit of Christ, he does not belong to Christ" (Romans 8:8–9).

Kindness is brought about in us only by the kindness shown to us through Jesus Christ. His kindness gives birth to kindness in us. His compassion gives birth to compassion in us.

Kindness is often misinterpreted! Some would say, "Kindness means tolerance of evil. It means leniency. It means being easy!" The truth of the matter is kindness means "telling it like it is" in a loving way. It means loving a teenager enough to say, "There is no such thing as safe sex!" It means teaching your little girl that honesty is the best policy despite what her friends may be telling her or what the world may be showing her. It means saying "no" and "never" and "not under this roof" even though it's not easy to do so.

Walking the Talk of Consistency

Few things are more confusing to young people today than the lack of consistency or commitment. "Here today, gone tomorrow," is too often a slogan describing many things—morals, absolutes, relationships, job security. Experts tell us that baby boomers (born between 1946 and 1964) and busters (born between 1965 and 1983) have become disillusioned with technology. It hasn't been the "promised savior." It has failed to produce any lasting security, any real happiness. In coming to the church, they ask, "Is this something we can depend on?"

Children need to know that though other things may seem to change with circumstances or time, God's Word never changes. It is the one thing we can and must depend on. "All men are like grass, and all their glory is like the flowers of the field; the grass withers and the flowers fall, but the Word of the Lord stands forever" (1 Peter 1:24–25).

We reflect to our children a picture of God in the way we treat them. In being consistent in the rules we offer and their consequences, we show them the consistency and truthfulness of God's rules and their consequences. When we inconsistently make rules and fail to administer the conse-

Notes:

quences for not following these rules, our children begin to wonder if the rules were really important.

Walking the Talk of Respect

One important definition of respect is "to look again …to look again and see that person through the eyes of God." In doing so, you say that a person is valuable. They count.

The world's view of respect is entirely different than God's. The world says, "I'll respect you as long as you deserve it." God respects His people even when they don't deserve it. Few sections of Scripture describe respect for us better than Romans 5:6–8:

"You see, at just the right time, when we were still powerless, Christ died for the ungodly. Very rarely will anyone die for a righteous man, though for a good man someone might possibly dare to die. But God demonstrates His own love for us in this: While we were still sinners, Christ died for us" (Romans 5:6–8).

Christ died for the ungodly! He died for His enemies. The world would say such people do not deserve respect! We didn't deserve Jesus' respect, yet He died for us.

Respecting means recognizing that each child may be different in temperament and personality. They may have different "love languages"—the way they express love. One may express his love in affirming words, another may express his love through physical touch. It means having high or special regard for each child. It means having good manners and common courtesy! It means treating them with the same respect you would treat your boss or some high government official.

Walking the Talk of Patience

To reflect a picture of God in the way we parent, it is extremely important for us to reflect patience. God is patient with us! St. Paul reminds us that "agape love," God-given love, is patient (1 Corinthians 13:4). In living "a life worthy of the calling you have received" one is to "be patient, bearing with one another in love" (Ephesians 4:1–2).

Notes:

Patience is no more natural than kindness or gentleness. The question then is, "How can one become more patient? Where does one get the needed patience to hear the long, silly story of your child which you've heard many times before?" Patience is a gift from the Holy Spirit. "But the fruit of the Spirit is … patience …" (Galatians 5:22). The Holy Spirit works through Word and Sacrament to strengthen faith so that you may be empowered with patience. John wrote, "The Spirit gives life; the flesh counts for nothing. The words I have spoken to you are spirit and they are life" (John 6:63). If we believe this to be true then wise parents will read and study God's Word daily. In searching the Word they will find "life" itself, even life filled with patience!

Walking the talk? As we discipline our children this week, we need to ask honestly of ourselves whether our walking the talk is filled with love, kindness, consistency and patience—important ingredients for the best of parenting.

Notes:

Opening Worship

Open the session by singing the hymn and reading the prayer in the study leaflet.

Hymn (see following page)

Day 1—Empowering Versus Controlling

1. a. James and John requested they receive position and power in this new kingdom established by God. One wanted to be seated on Jesus' right, another at His left (Mark 10:37). b. Matthew says the request was made by the mother of James and John (Matthew 20:20–21). Her name was Salome, and she was the sister to Mary, Jesus' mother, making James and John first cousins (Matthew 27:56, Mark 15:40, John 19:25). c. Both James and John would suffer for their faith. James was "put to death with the sword" (Acts 12:2). John was exiled to the "island of Patmos" because of his confession of faith (Revelation 1:9). d. Earthly greatness consists of power, wanting to dominate and lord over someone. Spiritual greatness consists of lowly and voluntary service (Mark 10:35–45).

2. Discipline is for the well being of the child. It empowers the child to be everything he/she can be. Without discipline there is little maturity.

3. Children who know that their input is important gain a feeling of worth and esteem. They see themselves as an integral part of the family.

4. Parents can listen to their children. They can try to build up each child taking into consideration each child's unique abilities. They can demonstrate forgiveness. Parents must see themselves as servants of God entrusted with children, called to serve.

Day 2—Positive Versus Negative

5. Unfortunately, most of us spend far more time speaking to our children when they're doing something wrong than when they're doing something right. Fortunately, it is an imbalance that can be corrected through some intentional hard work and time on our part.

6. a. St. Paul reminds us we are to think on those things that are "true, whatever is noble, whatever is right, whatever is pure, whatever is lovely, whatever is admirable—… is excellent or praiseworthy" (Philippians 4:8). b. The writer of Proverbs says "an anxious heart weighs a man down, but a kind word cheers him up" (Proverbs 12:25). c. The writer reminds us that "a gentle answer" is far better than a "harsh word." One "turns away wrath," the other "stirs up anger." d. Wise words are "like apples of gold in settings of silver." They make for a beautiful setting.

7. Give participants a moment to recall the negative and positive comments they last spoke to their children.

8. Allow for a time of reflection and prayer.

Day 3—Encouragement

9. a. St. Paul calls the Christians at Philippi "saints." The meaning of the word explains why this was a great compliment. It literally means those "who are set apart to live for God." They had been called to "live in holiness." b. St. Paul is thankful for the partnership they share in Christ Jesus. These words coming from St. Paul himself, a great leader in all of Christendom, were very encouraging to say the least. c. The Philippians had encouraged him not only with their prayers but also financially. Epaphroditus had recently

Holy Father, in Your Mercy

1 Ho - ly Fa - ther, in your mer - cy   Hear our anx - ious prayer;
2 Je - sus, Sav - ior, let your pres - ence   Be their light and guide;
3 When they sor - row, when in dan - ger,   When in lone - li - ness,
4 May the joy of your sal - va - tion   Be their strength and stay.
5 Ho - ly Spir - it, let your teach - ing   Sanc - ti - fy their life;
6 Fa - ther, Son, and Ho - ly Spir - it,   You are God a - lone;

Keep our loved ones who are ab - sent   In your care.
Keep, oh, keep them in their weak - ness   At your side.
In your love look down and com - fort   Their dis - tress.
May they love you, may they praise you   Day by day.
Send your grace that they may con - quer   In the strife.
Bless them, guide them, save them, keep them,   All you own.

Text: Isabella S. Stevenson, 1843-90, alt.
Tune: Henry W. Baker, 1821-77

STEPHANOS
85 83

brought supplies and other gifts to him (Philippians 4:18). d. St. Paul's prayer included requests for spiritual growth: "that your love may abound more and more in knowledge and depth of insight, so that you may be able to discern what is best and may be pure and blameless until the day of Christ, filled with the fruit of righteousness that comes through Jesus Christ—to the glory and praise of God" (Philippians 1:9–11). Our prayers are more often directed toward the physical well being of the child. e. The Holy Spirit produces in Christians "the fruit of righteousness." We can't produce these things in ourselves. Only the Holy Spirit can and does. Thus, Jesus identifies some of these "fruit of righteousness" in His Sermon on the Mount (Matthew 5:2–48). He produces far more within us than what the Law even demanded.

10. St. Paul spoke many words of encouragement along the way through the Macedonia area. These words must have included words of encouragement from Jesus Himself especially since so many of the people were so antagonistic toward Christianity, such as "Blessed are you when people insult you, persecute you" (Matthew 5:11).

11. We need to be sensitive of any in our group who might not be receiving much encouragement. If so, we pray for opportunities to share a word or deed of encouragement with them.

12. We can all improve on sharing our love with one another, including our children. Some of the ways might include rewards or speaking words of affirmation. Whatever you do, it is important you don't postpone speaking or doing these things before it's too late.

13. Everyone needs to be honest enough to take whatever responsibility he/she might have if the day doesn't turn out as Ziglar suggests. If yesterday wasn't everything you wanted it to be, pray that tomorrow God would empower you to do whatever you need to do to make it better.

14. Allow for a time of reflection and prayer.

Day 4—Unconditional Love

15. a. The term "eros" refers to erotic love. It is sexual in nature. The term "philia" denotes friendship. Both terms denote love that is possessing and deserving. b. "Agape" love is undeserved. It is love that gives and gives. It is best expressed in Romans 5:8, "But God demonstrates His own love for us in this: While we were still sinners, Christ died for us" (Romans 5:8). c. "Agape" love is many things. It is "patient … kind … does not envy … does not boast … is not proud … is not rude … is not self-seeking … is not easily angered … keeps no record of wrongs … does not delight in evil … but rejoices with the truth … it protects … trusts … hopes … preserves … never fails" (1 Corinthians 13:4–8). d. "Agape" love is by nature eternal because it is from God. "God is love" (1 John 4:16b). e. St. Paul reminds us that "agape" love is not a child kind of love. It isn't conditional. It isn't filled with qualifications.

16. Whenever we make our love for our child based on what the child does instead of who she/he is, we are saying, "You're valuable as long as you perform or act a certain way."

17. Have the group discuss different verbal and behavioral ways they have shown affection to their children in the last week.

18. Grace is an integral part of "agape" love because it is undeserved. St. Paul reminds us that we have been saved by grace. It was God's doing totally, not ours (Ephesians 2:8–9).

19. If the house is a "grace place" it is filled with unconditional love. It is a place where people feel free enough to confess their sins, knowing there is forgiveness. It is a place of strong commitment to God and to one another.

Day 5—Nurture from the Church Community

Christianity is about relationships. Relationships were broken by sin, but with Christ relationships were restored, not only between God and people but also between people.

20. a. St. Paul reminds the Thessalonians to "encourage one another and build each other up" (1 Thessalonians 5:11). He wanted them to be united in helping one another. b. In Galatians 6:10 Paul reminds us we are to "do good to all people, especially to those who belong to the family of believers" (Galatians 6:10). c. The fellowship of believers as described in Acts 2:42–47 demonstrates the great concern and care Christians should have for one another. "All the believers were together and had everything in common" (Acts 2:44).

21. The village—the church—helps raise the child of each person in the congregation by providing everything from Sunday school to a youth group. People of the village, or the church, are concerned for each fellow member because each member is valuable—a part of them!

22. There are many things we can do to be better "pathfinders" for the youth and children of our congregation. It always begins by walking the talk. Children watch adults. They want to know that what is being said is also being lived. Congregations can help by providing educational opportunities to enrich marriages and families. They can ask what the needs of their families are by surveying the congregation and then responding to those needs.

23. Allow for a time of reflection and prayer.

Lecture—Session 4

Building Up One Another

Listen to these phrases. How do they make you feel?

- "Way to go!"
- "Good for you!"
- "You're the best!"
- "I never did that well when I was your age."
- "I'm impressed."
- "That's my boy/girl!"
- "I love you."
- "You're a 10 plus!"
- "You never fail to amaze me."
- "We are so proud of you."
- "Have you ever improved!"
- "You're number one in my book."

Good parenting requires the art of affirmation. Abraham Lincoln said, "A drop of honey catches more flies than a gallon of gall." Mark Twain said, "I can live for two months on one good compliment." Research has shown repeatedly that encouragement is the best way to inspire children to do better.

Parenting that Empowers

In one of our earlier lectures we talked about "empowering" a child, meaning we want to help our child become everything he/she can. Jesus Christ "empowers" His people. We are empowered by the Holy Spirit working through Word and Sacrament! Jesus tells us, "I have come that they may have life, and have it to the full" (John 10:10). John writes, "Yet to all who received Him, to those who believed in His name, He gave the right to become children of God—children born not of natural descent, nor of human decision or a husband's will, but born of God" (John 1:12–13). Think about it. We who were powerless and sinful, He has made His children. "How great is the love the Father has lavished on us, that we should be called children of God" (1 John 3:1). As His children we share His very power (Ephesians 1:19).

Disciplining a child is one way to empower a child. A child who knows no boundaries or has little respect for other people will not fare very well in the world either as a child or as an adult. To empower a child takes time. It means taking time to listen to the child's stories. It means appreciating and affirming the child's uniqueness. It means forgiving and being forgiven. It means even allowing the child to choose certain behaviors and then suffer the consequences to learn a valuable lesson.

Unfortunately, some parents hold on to their children too tightly. This hinders the children from becoming everything they can be. Parents who do this will even rationalize, "It's for the good of the child." Balswick writes:

"Many times … the child is kept in a dependent position for the parent's own convenience. Empowering is the ultimate goal, where parents release the child to self-control. Of course, mistakes will be made, and failure, will be an occasional consequence of trying out new wings. Parent have a hard time letting their children make mistakes (especially the same mistakes they themselves made when young), so this is a difficult transition for parents and children alike. It is important to remind parents that the key to their authority lies not in external control, but rather in internal control which their children can integrate into their own personhood. When this happens, it is a rewarding and mutually satisfying achievement." (*The Family*, by Jack Balswick and Judith Balswick, Baker Book House, Grand Rapids, Mich., 1991.)

Parents who empower their children reflect the empowerment the Holy Spirit provides to us through God's Word to us. To empower is to parent wisely.

Parenting with the Positive

Throughout Scripture we are reminded that we are to accentuate the positive. Passage after passage in the book of Proverbs tells us the benefits of encouragement:

"An anxious heart weighs a man down, but a kind word cheers him up" (Proverbs 12:25).

Notes:

"A gentle answer turns away wrath, but a harsh word stirs up anger" (Proverbs 15:1).

"The tongue has the power of life and death, and those who love it will eat its fruit" (Proverbs 18:21).

"A word aptly spoken is like apples of gold in settings of silver" (Proverbs 25:11).

St. Paul writes to the Philippians:

"Finally, brothers, whatever is true, whatever is noble, whatever is right, whatever is pure, whatever is lovely, whatever is admirable—if anything is excellent or praiseworthy—think about such things" (Philippians 4:8).

Life itself was conceived through the Word of God. "By the word of the LORD were the heavens made … For He spoke, and it came to be; He commanded, and it stood firm" (Psalm 33:6, 9). We share in God's creative work when we give life to our children through our positive words.

Parenting with Encouragement

William James wrote, "The deepest principle in human nature is the craving to be appreciated." Every person needs encouragement. Since children need to know that they are appreciated, parents need to examine their "praise giving." Does it surpass their "criticism giving"? The more secure children feel about themselves the more confident they will be. Zig Ziglar reminds us, "If you start your day lovingly and gently with your child and end the day the same way, you'll eliminate a lot of trouble between the two events." (*Raising Positive Kids in a Negative World*, by Zig Ziglar, Ballantine Books, New York, 1989.)

Scripture talks about the importance of using God's Word to encourage and build up one another. "Now I commit you to God and to the word of His grace, which can build you up and give you an inheritance among all those who are sanctified" (Acts 20:32). Christians can truly build up one another! The Word of God reminds us that we have great value, value given to us through Jesus' death and resurrection. "Once you were not a people, but now you are the people of God" (1 Peter 2:10).

Notes:

There's a story of a young man who had been taken from his home in Africa to become a slave in America. He along with many others spent months on a crowded ship filled with disease and rotten food. When arriving in America he was placed on a platform to be sold to the highest bidder. This young man, however, was much different than the others. He stood proud, his chest forward glistening in the sun, his chin upward, his eyes glowing. When asked why this man was so different, the slave trader called out, "He is the son of a great king in Africa, and he cannot forget it."

So every child needs to know he/she is the son or daughter of a great king, the King of kings, God Himself. What words could be more encouraging than "You were bought at a price" (1 Corinthians 6:20) or "He who did not spare His own Son, but gave Him up for us all—how will He not also, along with Him, graciously give us all things" (Romans 8:32)? Helen Keller said, "So much has been given to me, I have no time to ponder over that which has been denied." Wise parents will let their children know that they are valuable.

Parenting with Love

A key to parenting is to love unconditionally, just as God loves unconditionally. True love is eternal because it is from God. "God is love" (1 John 4:16b), and He is eternal. "Love never fails," writes St. Paul. Other things will fail, but real love doesn't, meaning it goes on and on.

When parents love conditionally they show children an inaccurate picture of God's love. The child reasons, "The only way I can be loved is to perform or act in a certain way!" We know God's love is just the opposite: "Christ died for the ungodly" (Romans 5:6). Children need to know they are loved by God and us despite their "ungodly" behavior at times. They need to feel free to confess their sins, knowing that there is forgiveness.

Parenting with the Help of Others

St. Paul writes: "Therefore encourage one another and build each other up, just as in fact you are doing" (1 Thessalonians 5:11). The word "build" applies to building houses. Parents are in the business of "building" future generations as they

Notes:

prepare their children and children's children to continue doing God's work here on earth. The task is overwhelming. It is for this reason God gives to us others who can help us, especially within the church.

Throughout the Scriptures there are examples of people who mentored others, who helped encourage and guide others. Eli mentored young Samuel. Moses mentored Joshua. Barnabas mentored Paul. Paul mentored Timothy. Mentors are "pathfinders," meaning they help others stay on the right path. Wise parents will connect their children to others who can mentor them, who will support the values they themselves as parents hold to and are trying to teach their children. These connections include adult friends, peers, and church family.

Few things are as challenging in life as parenting. However, we are reminded in Scripture that we can meet the challenges as we remember to parent with the goal of empowering, as we parent with the positive, as we parent with encouragement, as we parent with love, and as we parent with the help of others.

Notes:

Opening Worship

Open the session by singing the hymn and reading the prayer in the study leaflet.

Hymn (see following page)

Day 1—The Law as a Curb

1. When we think of the word "law," many things come to mind. We might think of the civil laws of the land (e.g., "The speed limit is 65 miles per hour"), or we may think of the moral law of God (e.g., "Thou shall not kill"). Laws and the obedience of them are necessary or there is chaos. A society without laws is like an essay without punctuation.

2. One of the primary reasons God gave His family rules was to "control violent outbursts of sin and keep order in the world." (*Luther's Small Catechism*, CPH, St. Louis, Mo., 1986, p. 94.) St. Paul reminded Timothy that the Law acts as a curb to hold back and keep in check coarse outbursts of sin (1 Timothy 1:9, 10). He also reminds us in Romans 2:14–15 that the Gentiles guided by their conscience, did know and practice some of the Mosaic laws. Thus, the Law with its threat of punishment acts as a curb.

3. a. The Ten Commandments codify acceptable human behavior. For centuries they have helped curb misbehavior. Take for example, "You shall not murder." What would a society be like without obedience to such a law? The results of disobedience are obvious. b. These commandments are not just God's suggestions, they are His commandments. They spell out clearly what He demands of His people. If they were mere suggestions people would have an option of whether or not they chose to follow them. People are commanded to follow them.

4. The reason why "kids cheat more … steal more

… curse more" is obvious. Parents have tried to rear their children without the Judeo-Christian Law. Without some reference to God's Law, everything parents teach becomes subjective and based on what they believe instead of what God has placed on their hearts.

5. There are many creative and fun ways of studying the Mosaic Law with your children. You might make a game out of memorizing the commandments or you might discuss with your children as you're driving down the street how God's Law serves as a curb.

Day 2—The Law as a Mirror

6. The Law serves as a mirror for God's people because, as Martin Luther wrote, "The Law accuses us and shows us our sin" (*Luther's Small Catechism*, CPH, St. Louis, Mo., 1986, p. 95). It breaks down man's self-sufficiency and pride, reminding him that he cannot make himself righteous before God.

7. a. Paul reminds us in Romans 3:19–20 that the Law serves as a mirror for both the Gentiles as well as the Jews. It shows us we sin daily and need forgiveness. b. In Romans 7:7, St. Paul reminds us that the Law reveals the presence and fact of sin.

8. a. There are many rationalizations used to attempt to cover up sin. For example, homosexuality is no longer called a sin, it is now simply an "alternate lifestyle." Instead of using the word "abortion" for the act of killing a baby we simply say, "terminating a pregnancy." b. It is obvious why society finds truth as revealed in God's Word so often too strong a medicine to digest undiluted. Truth convicts. It reminds us that before God we are not right! c. The media—television,

Just as I am, Without One Plea

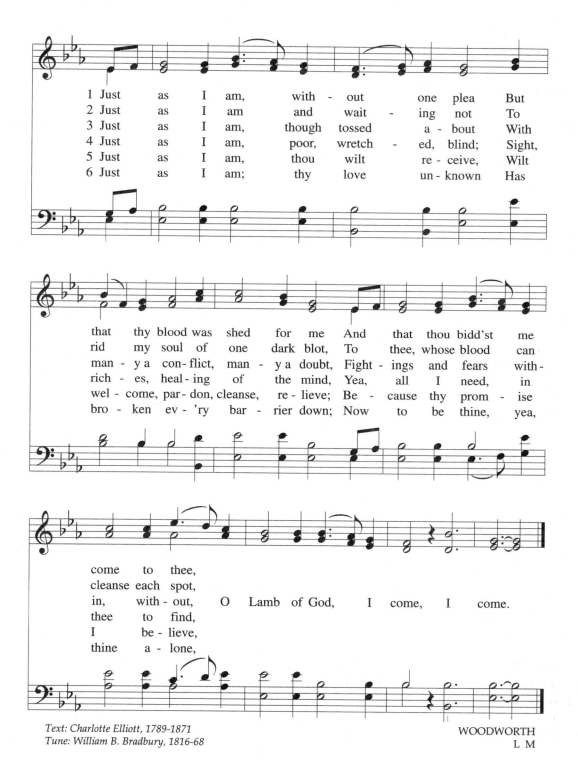

1 Just as I am, with - out one plea But
2 Just as I am and wait - ing not To
3 Just as I am, though tossed a - bout With
4 Just as I am, poor, wretch - ed, blind; Sight,
5 Just as I am, thou wilt re - ceive, Wilt
6 Just as I am; thy love un - known Has

that thy blood was shed for me And that thou bidd'st me
rid my soul of one dark blot, To thee, whose blood can
man - y a con - flict, man - y a doubt, Fight - ings and fears with -
rich - es, heal - ing of the mind, Yea, all I need, in
wel - come, par - don, cleanse, re - lieve; Be - cause thy prom - ise
bro - ken ev - 'ry bar - rier down; Now to be thine, yea,

come to thee,
cleanse each spot,
in, with - out, O Lamb of God, I come, I come.
thee to find,
I be - lieve,
thine a - lone,

Text: Charlotte Elliott, 1789-1871
Tune: William B. Bradbury, 1816-68

WOODWORTH
L M

movies—make our job as parents more and more difficult in defining for our children what sin actually is. So often prime-time television programs teach our children values contrary to what we teach them.

9. Without the Gospel there is no hope. St. Paul experienced the same thing we do; "For what I do is not the good I want to do; no, the evil I do not want to do—this I keep on doing" (Romans 7:19). So where did He find hope? The same place we do; "Thanks be to God—through Jesus Christ our Lord!" (Romans 7:25)

10. Allow for a time of silent prayer.

Day 3—The Law as a Guide

11. Christians cannot on their own keep the commands of God. Though the Law serves as a wonderful guide, because of their sinfulness people are unable to use the Law as a guide. However, because Christians are "under grace," not the Law, they are empowered by the Holy Spirit to use the Law as a guide (Romans 6:14).

12. a. God's Law to Christians directs and guides them by pointing out what is good and pleasing in the sight of God. Transformed by the Holy Spirit, the Christians are empowered to obedient service—"able to test and approve what God's will is—His good, pleasing and perfect will" (Romans 12:2). b. The psalmist reminds us that "a young man keep(s) his way pure … by living according to (God's) Word" (Psalm 119:9). This is possible only through faith in Jesus Christ. c. Micah says there are three things a God-fearing person does: (1) "to act justly"; (2) "to love mercy"; and (3) "to walk humbly with … God" (Micah 6:8). d. As God has loved us through Jesus Christ, so "we also ought to love one another" (1 John 4:11).

13. Disobedience of God's Law eventually leads to despair. A "peace … which transcends all understanding" comes from being in relationship with God and with others. Through faith in Jesus Christ, we have such a relationship with God and with others. Out of love for our God we respond with love that leads to real "harmony and inner peace."

14. Have the group discuss how the Law was used in their homes while growing up.

15. Whatever use of the Law you feel you need to use more of, remember the Law by itself never changes a person. Only the Gospel of Jesus Christ changes people. The Law convicts us. Only through faith in Jesus Christ can we respond to the Law.

Day 4—The Power of the Gospel

16. a. The religious leaders of that day were criticizing Jesus for hobnobbing and eating with "tax collectors and sinners" (Luke 15:2). b. The father did not lay down the law and forbid his son to go away with his inheritance because he knew all the law in the world wouldn't have changed his mind, or if it did, he would have had a son who was terribly rebellious and difficult to live with. c. The son came to recognize his desperation. He recognized his sin and how foolish he was (Luke 15:17–18). d. Remind participants of the formula suggested in another lesson—five affirmations for every criticism. e. The Gospel is our heavenly Father loving us despite our sinfulness, because God's own Son willingly gave up His life on the cross to pay for our sin—sin that had at one time separated us from God. He asks no questions. He simply welcomes us back, as St. Paul reminds us, "But God demonstrates His own love for us in this: While we were still sinners, Christ died for us" (Romans 5:8).

17. The "thou shalt" of the Law was replaced by the power of the Gospel—grace (Romans 6:14). The Christian is free from the Law as a ladder to heaven. The Law could not enable them to be righteous. It only convicted them. The Law continues to convict us, but the Gospel—grace—enables us to live God-pleasing lives.

18. All three statements (a, b, c) are true. C.F.W. Walther in his 25th thesis on Law and Gospel, says that the Gospel is to predominate over the Law. It is important though that both Law and Gospel be preached and that we find ourselves to be both saints and sinners simultaneously.

19. Allow for a time of reflection and prayer.

Day 5—God-Directed Results

20. a. Those directed by the sinful nature are filled with "sexual immorality, impurity and debauchery, idolatry and witchcraft, hatred, discord, jealousy, fits of rage, selfish ambition, dissensions, factions and envy; drunkenness, orgies, and the like" (Galatians 5:19–21). Those led by the Spirit are filled with "love, joy, peace, patience, kindness, goodness, faithfulness, gentleness and self-control (Galatians 5:22–23). b. When one is led by the Spirit he/she is no longer under the Law, meaning his/her relationship with God isn't dependent on how well he/she keeps the Law. Instead, it's based on what Christ did for him/her. c. A person who is led by the Spirit, walks in the Spirit. He continues by the Spirit to live as God desires.

21. Have the group discuss which of the fruit are most and least obvious in their homes.

22. St. Paul told Timothy that God even had purpose in showing such great patience with him, such a major sinner of his day. It was to serve as an example and an encouragement for others to put their trust in Christ Jesus. Unfortunately, as parents we often don't stack up very well against God and the patience He shows us repeatedly. For this and all other sins we rely solely upon the grace of God revealed in the person and work of Jesus.

23. Lead the group in praying Galatians 5:22–23.

Lecture—Session 5

A Home that Is a "Grace Place"

There is a story of a hunter who raised his rifle and took careful aim at a large bear. Just as he was about to pull the trigger the bear spoke to him in a soft voice, "Sir, why don't we talk about this first? What is it that you want? Let's negotiate to see if we can work something out."

The hunter was shocked. He lowered his rifle and replied, "What I really want is a fur coat."

"Okay, let's talk. What do you want?" asked the hunter.

"I just want a full stomach. Why don't we negotiate a compromise?"

So they sat down and they negotiated. A short while later the bear walked away alone. The negotiations had taken place with some success. The bear had a full stomach. The hunter had his fur coat.

Though it is valuable to negotiate, sometimes negotiations get people into trouble. Obedience is often negotiated: "I'll do this if you'll do this, otherwise forget it." People often get around commandments, rules, and regulations through a variety of loopholes. What at one time was a sin is now considered only an alternate lifestyle! Sometimes people simply negotiate to keep from having to take responsibility. The truth of the matter is boundaries, laws, rules, and regulations are necessary for ordered living! These are necessary to survive. In today's world, few rules are absolutes. Everything is debatable. God entrusts parents with the responsibility of teaching His rules of living to their children without negotiating; "Impress them on your children. Talk about them when you sit at home and when you walk along the road, when you lie down and when you get up" (Deuteronomy 6:7).

The Law and Its Purpose

God gave man His Law—the Ten Commandments. They outline the way He wants us to live. God wrote this Law on our hearts, but because of sin, knowledge of that Law became blurred and there was little, if any, obedience of it. Later God arranged the Law in Ten Commandments, revealing these laws to His people, through Moses His prophet.

Though these Ten Commandments can no longer be taught in public schools or posted in court hallways, nevertheless, they are as true today as they were when God originally gave them to us. God entrusts us with the responsibility of teaching these commandments to our children. As we do, the commandments serve a three-fold purpose: (1) to serve as a curb; (2) to serve as a mirror; and, (3) to serve as a guide.

The Law as a Curb

Freida was a 90-year-old woman who refused to join the "Golden Agers Club" at the church because she said, "That club is only for old people." One of the hardest things I had to do as her pastor was to convince her to give up driving. However, it became apparent I had no choice after she had invited my wife and I to join her for Sunday brunch. She insisted she drive us in her '57 Chevy. The brunch was at a luxurious hotel. Following the brunch, the parking valet brought her car to the entrance of the hotel, and we all got in to drive away. Freida somehow missed seeing where the street began and the curb ended. We found ourselves driving with two wheels on the curb smashing every water sprinkler along the street. I looked into the rear view mirror to see the parking valet running after us as Freida destroyed one sprinkler after another. We finally hit the street with a large jolt. Freida laughed and said, "Pastor, I don't understand why they don't clean these streets a little better."

The curb was there to keep Freida off the grassy area and away from the sprinklers. More importantly curbs protect pedestrians walking on the sidewalk. The Law also protects and acts to curb "violent outbursts of sin and keep order in the world." (*Luther's Small Catechism*, CPH, St. Louis, Mo., 1986.)

The Law of God cannot serve as a curb if parents do not train their children in the Law. Too often today, parents see God's Law as only suggestions. They are more than suggestions. They are the *Law*. They curb sin. If sin is left unchecked, it eventually destroys.

Maybe one reason there is so much violence and crime today is because too often God's absolutes haven't been taught. Everything is subjective. God gives us clear absolutes in His commandments. There is no room for loopholes!

The Law as a Mirror

Today people play "The Blame Game." It's always someone else's fault or the circumstances that made me do what I did. Everyone talks about rights and few about responsibility. We color sin with slogans, euphemisms, and rationalizations. God calls us to be responsible, to confess our sin, to recognize who we are before God because of our sin!

God gave us the Law as a mirror to help us see ourselves as we really are. When we share God's laws with our children we help them see themselves as they really are. St. Paul exclaimed: "I do not understand what I do. For what I want to do I do not do, but what I hate I do … What a wretched man I am! Who will rescue me from this body of death? Thanks be to God—through Jesus Christ our Lord!" (Romans 7:15, 24–25). The Law shows us that we sin daily and need the forgiveness only Jesus can provide.

A Christian parent can say to their children: "What I'm sharing with you is from God Himself. These words don't change with time or with how we might feel at a certain time, they're as true today as when I was a child. They come from God, a God who loves us enough to give us guidelines by which to live." The media, television and movies, would try to present a different picture to our children: "Do what comes naturally." "Everyone else is doing it." Children will never really know what they look like before God because of sin unless they know God's Law. Children will never recognize their need for their Savior, Jesus Christ, until they see the enormity of their sin. Children will never experience the joy of Christ's forgiveness until they confess the sin they see in the mirror.

The Law as a Guide

As Christians we use the Law as a guide. We who have been regenerated through faith in Christ are free from the bondage of the Law. Jesus Christ fulfilled the Law in our stead, because we were unable to fulfill it on our own. Now motivated by God's love in Jesus, we desire to please Him. The

Notes:

Law of God guides and directs us on how we can do that. Any obedience to the Law flows from faith, the obedience of a loved child of God. We obey because we desire to. We cannot obey on our own. God enables us to obey through the power of the Holy Spirit.

One parent said:

"My child doesn't need to believe in God to believe that there are certain rights and wrongs that she must subscribe to. I teach her that her moral standards must be based on what is good for people. She must not treat people in any way that she herself would not want to be treated … no cheating, lying, physical or verbal abusing."

Though this may sound good, the truth of the matter is unless children have a standard, some specific guidelines, it is not always easy for them to determine what "is good for people." Hitler convinced people his actions were for the good of the people! Look at the tragic results of that kind of reasoning. Far better for us and our children that we don't have to guess what's "good for people." We can rely on God Himself who created all people and sent His only Son to all people. God lays out clearly in His Word the things that are good for those He created.

The Power Is in the Gospel

Recall St. Paul's words: "What a wretched man I am! Who will rescue me from this body of death? Thanks be to God—through Jesus Christ our Lord!" (Romans 7:24–25). The Law never changes people. It can convict. It can serve as a curb. It can guide. Only the Gospel of Jesus Christ changes hearts. The Gospel "is the power of God" (Romans 1:16). God's love in Christ enables Christian homes to be a "grace place," a place where God's love is spoken of and demonstrated in actions.

As parents, we need to examine our use of the Law versus the Gospel in our homes. How often do we use the Law compared to the Gospel? The Gospel is about grace and love. It's about forgiveness.

The home that is a "grace place" looks like this: it is filled with "love, joy, peace, patience, kindness, goodness, faithfulness, gentleness and self-control" (Galatians 5:22–23).

Notes:

Opening Worship

Open the session by singing the hymn and reading the prayer in the study leaflet.

Hymn (see following page)

Day 1—When Logical and Natural Consequences Don't Work

1. a. Logical consequences are those that are logical to the person experiencing them. If a child refuses to keep her room clean, a logical consequence might be to hire a cleaning lady and take the cleaning fee out of the child's allowance. b. Natural consequences are those that are the natural result of a person's behavior. If a child refuses to bring his comics in from outside even though he's been told repeatedly by his parents to do so, he may have to suffer the consequences of seeing his comics get ruined.

2. a. God was willing to go to great lengths to bring Jonah back to his senses. He sends a big fish to swallow Jonah and throw him up onto the land to once again be given the chance to do the task God set before him to do (Jonah 1:15–17; 3:1–2). b. The great fish was a way God used to bring Jonah back to his senses. Some may consider it a punishment for Jonah's disobedience; however, it was appointed by God to retrieve Jonah and bring him back to the task God wanted him to do. c. Just as Jonah was in the belly of the whale for three days and three nights so the Son of Man, Jesus Christ, would be "in the heart of the earth" (Matthew 12:40). Just as Jonah was spewed out of the belly of the whale to preach a message of salvation, so the Son of Man would be resurrected from the grave and bring the good news of salvation to all people.

3. Proper perspective comes in answer to prayer. Jonah ultimately sees that God was behind his circumstances. James reminds us that we are to pray for such wisdom in difficult situations as well (James 1:5).

4. Allow the participants to share any particularly difficult discipline situations they've experienced. Pray for wisdom and discernment in handling these situations.

Day 2—When There's Sibling Rivalry

5. a. Joseph had more than likely reported negatively about his brothers to his father. He was now being asked once again to "go and see" how his brothers were doing (Genesis 37:14). b. Joseph was adorned with a "richly ornamented robe" indicating favoritism (Genesis 37:23). It appeared that Joseph did not hide the fact that he was liked by his father. Favoritism was something that ran in the family since Jacob was favored more than Esau by Rebekah his mother (Genesis 25:28). c. Answers will vary.

6. Allow participants to share their experiences with sibling rivalry.

7. Discuss the expert statements. Do the participants agree or disagree?

8. Prayer alone won't change the situation; however, it is clear from Scripture that we are to ask boldly in the name of Jesus and He'll hear and answer (Matthew 21:22; James 1:6–7). Along with prayer we must use the discipline techniques experts have shown to be useful.

Day 3—Temper Tantrums

9. Temper tantrums have many different faces. A child may throw himself on the floor and scream. He can pout, withdraw and not say anything, in an attempt to punish everyone around him. She may break something or even hold her breath!

Come, My Soul, with Every Care

1 Come, my soul, with ev-'ry care, Je - sus loves to an - swer prayer;
2 You are com-ing to your King, Large pe - ti - tions with you bring;
3 With my bur-den I be - gin: Lord, re-move this load of sin;
4 Lord, your rest to me im - part, Take pos - ses - sion of my heart;
5 While I am a pil-grim here, Let your love my spir - it cheer;
6 Show me what I am to do; Ev - 'ry hour my strength re - new.

He him-self bids you to pray, There-fore will not turn a - way.
For his grace and pow'r are such None can ev - er ask too much.
Let your blood, for sin - ners split, Set my con-science free from guilt.
There your blood-bought right main - tain And with-out a ri - val reign.
As my guide, my guard, my friend, Lead me to my jour-ney's end.
Let me live a life of faith; Let me die your peo - ple's death.

Text: John Newton, 1725-1807, alt.
Tune: Justin Heinrich Knecht, 1752-1817

VIENNA
7 7 7 7

10. a. The son's temper tantrum looked a lot like someone who is sulking or pouting. He refused to even go to the celebration (Luke 15:28). b. The elder son represents the Pharisees and teachers of the law who hated Jesus. c. The elder son doesn't even acknowledge the prodigal son as his brother, he simply refers to him as "this son of yours" (Luke 15:30). d. The father reasons with the son. He explains to his older son why he is treating his younger son as he is. Good communication that brings about understanding is essential not only for helping with temper tantrums but in dealing with any discipline problem.

11. The father was able to control himself and not add fuel to the fire by yelling or arguing. He simply explained the situation and his reason for doing what he did. When a parent yells, argues, or loses control of himself, he may even be promoting future arguments between siblings.

12. There are many suggestions that are useful when a child pouts. Certainly, one thing is not to pay attention to a child who's pouting. That's what he wants—attention. One might want to quietly tell him to go to his room if he's going to pout because no one wants to see how unpleasant he's looking at this time.

Day 4—Testing

13. Children test their parents in order to get what they want. If you don't give them what they want, their goal may be to hurt you like you've hurt them.

14. a. The woman tried to get Jesus steered away from the conversation at hand. She asked questions that had nothing to do with what they were talking. For example, in verse 20 she said, "Our fathers worshiped on this mountain, but you Jews claim that the place where we must worship is in Jerusalem." Whenever the conversation got uncomfortable she tried to turn it around in another direction. b. Much like a child, the woman simply asked questions, such as, "Are you greater than our father Jacob?" and "Where should people worship?" (John 4:12, 20). c. Jesus was skillful as a communicator. He kept steering her in the direction she needed to go to recognize

her need for a Savior. The woman obviously made a powerful testimony of what happened at the well and, because of this testimony, many Samaritans believed (John 4:39).

15. Some other forms of testing or manipulation include threats, physically running away, playing the martyr, and intimidating.

16. A child will have one or two favorite techniques because they work. He/she won't waste his/her time using what doesn't work after a while.

17. We all need encouragement from time to time. St. Paul reminds us, "Let us not become weary in doing good, for at the proper time we will reap a harvest if we do not give up" (Galatians 6:9).

Day 5—Perfection

18. a. The other priest being spoken of—"one in the order of Melchizedek"—was Jesus Christ Himself (Hebrews 7:11, 22). b. The Levitical priesthood, the law of Moses, was unable to save people because people could not keep this law perfectly, as they were required. Another priest was needed, one who could make us perfect. Only Jesus Christ could do that through His own life, death, and resurrection.

19. There'll be a new heaven and a new earth, perfect as it was in the Garden of Eden. There will be no more imperfection—"no more death or mourning or crying or pain, for the old order of things has passed away" (Revelation 21:4). There'll be no more testing, no more manipulation, no more …!

20. Invite the participants to exchange phone numbers so they can continue to pray for and encourage one another. Close with prayer.

Lecture—Session 6

Special Discipline Concerns

There's a helpful parenting program by Thomas W. Phelan entitled, *1-2-3 Magic*. It offers an effective method for managing the behavior of children from the ages of two to 10 years of age. Basically the program goes like this:

"Imagine your child is doing something you don't want him to do, such as complaining:

1. You calmly give a warning that is both verbal and visual. Holding up one finger, you say, "That's 1."

2. If he stops, fine. If he doesn't, you give a second verbal and visual warning. Holding up two fingers, you say, "That's 2."

3. If he stops, great. If he doesn't, you hold up three fingers and say, "That's 3, take 5." He then has to go to his room for five minutes. When he comes out you act as if nothing had happened—no lectures and no apologies—and you repeat the procedure whenever necessary." (*1-2-3 Magic!*, *Effective Discipline for Children* by Thomas W. Phelan, Child Management Inc., Glen Ellyn, IL, 1-800-442-4453.)

In California, there is a new law called "Three Strikes and You're Out." If you commit a felony three times, you're in jail for life.

There's an interesting parallel between the parenting program entitled *1-2-3 Magic*, the California penal code of "Three Strikes and You're Out," and the story of Peter denying Jesus three times (John 18:15–18; 25–27).

Three times Peter denied knowing Jesus. Do you think Jesus glanced in Peter's direction and with His look told him to "take five," to go home and await the news? His death was imminent. Jesus had clearly told him He had to die in order to redeem all people.

The good news was that Peter didn't strike out with Jesus! Jesus gave him a second chance to confess his love and allegiance to Him. When appearing to the disciples after His resurrection Jesus took Peter aside and asked him three times, "Simon son of John, do you truly love Me more than these?" (John 21:15), and three times Peter answered back, "Yes, Lord, You know that I love You" (John 21:16). The great lover of our souls, Jesus Christ, invited Peter back into a relationship with Him.

Jesus continued to love Peter even after Peter denied knowing Him. Throughout Scripture, we see how God continued to love His children even after they threw temper tantrums or threatened Him, even though they tested and tried to manipulate Him. In a like manner, even when we are challenged with an especially difficult child—one who may be an expert in manipulation or testing—we remain dedicated to love the child.

When Challenged by Sibling Rivalry

Sibling rivalry is a common problem in many homes. Examples of such rivalry abound in Scripture; Cain and Abel, Jacob and Esau, Joseph and his brothers. Scripture records some of the reasons for such rivalry. For example, "Isaac, who had a taste for wild game, loved Esau, but Rebekah loved Jacob" (Genesis 25:28). Favoritism only further heightened the sibling rivalry between the twin brothers.

Empirical research has recently shown what Scripture has always told us; "The prayer of a righteous man is powerful and effective" (James 5:16). Prayer works in healing people physically and emotionally. For example, it was discovered that, without exception, every couple in a marriage counseling group who agreed to pray together for at least 15 minutes a day were helped tremendously. For the majority of couples, healing came to their relationships. If prayer helps heal troubled marriages, couldn't it also help siblings who argue and fight? What if parents stopped arguing and fighting about who started it or whose fault it was and simply gathered everyone involved to pray? We might begin by asking that each party remain silent for a moment and think about what has happened. Invite them to join hands with you. Take the lead in asking for forgiveness for any ill feelings we have toward one another. Then rejoice in the forgiveness God offers through Jesus. Ask for God's help in bringing peace into the home. The prayers can vary. As everyone becomes more comfortable praying at these times, you might even ask the two siblings to confess his/her own sins and failures which have brought about the rivalry. When this happens, be sure to celebrate God's forgiveness. As the parent you might even want to place your hand on each sibling and announce the forgiveness that is theirs through Jesus Christ.

Notes:

When Challenged by Temper Tantrums

Temper tantrums are common among most children age two and up. A temper tantrum has many faces. It can be a three-year-old throwing himself on the floor. It can be a girl pounding on her door after being sent to her room to cool down. It can be a child holding his breath.

A classic example of someone who had a temper tantrum is the older son in the well known story of the Prodigal Son. "The older brother became angry and refused to go in" (Luke 15:28). He threw a temper tantrum. He pouted and refused to participate in the family celebration. He even refused to call his brother "my brother." Instead he spoke contemptuously of his brother as "this son of yours" (Luke 15:30).

In the story of the Prodigal Son, the father didn't lose his cool. He did not yell or argue. He calmly explained the situation (Luke 15:31–32). In a similar way, when we can calmly reflect on a situation we can create an environment for healthy communication, a peaceful solution to sibling rivalry, or an atmosphere for the successful conclusion to a temper tantrum.

One effective method of dealing with a temper tantrum is the model suggested at the very beginning of this lecture—*1-2-3 Magic*. It involves no discussion on fault or any long lectures, it simply calls for time out. If five minutes doesn't work, additional time might be needed.

When Challenged by Testing

Dr. Phelan counsels parents to remember that most kids will not thank them for disciplining them. It would be rare to hear a child say, "I want to thank you dad for giving me 10 minutes out. It felt good." Instead they'll test and manipulate us in an attempt to either get what they want or to punish us for not giving in to them. (*1-2-3 Magic!, Effective Discipline for Children* by Thomas W. Phelan, Child Management Inc., Glen Ellyn, IL, 1-800-442-4453.)

Often people tried to manipulate Jesus. The woman at the well tried to manipulate Him:

"Are You (really) greater than our father Jacob, who gave us the well and drank from it himself, as did also his sons and his flocks and herds?" (John 4:12).

"Our fathers worshiped on this mountain, but you Jews claim that the place where we must worship is in Jerusalem" (John 4:20).

Jesus kept directing her back to the real issue at hand so that she might experience His love and forgiveness.

Children who manipulate can try to sidetrack us. They attempt to lead us astray, causing us to lose our focus on what the real issues might be. As parents we need to ask ourselves whether or not we are getting baited or sidetracked. As long as a child sees his mission being accomplished, he will continue doing it over and over again.

Perfection

Though we may acknowledge perfection is never to be achieved here on earth, often our actions would suggest that we believe something else. Unrealistic expectations lead to disillusionment for not only children but also for parents. Do we sometimes expect our children to think and reason like adults? When they don't do what we expect of them do we intimidate, or pout, or threaten? If so, why should they act any different? St. Paul writes: "When I was a child, I talked like a child, I thought like a child, I reasoned like a child. When I became a man, I put childish ways behind me" (1 Corinthians 13:11). It should be every parent's prayer that they put away any childish ways of handling conflict and act like adults.

Parents may even beat themselves up if their children go awry, lamenting "What did we do wrong?" The truth of the matter is, you may have parented as well as the next door neighbor whose children turned out so well adjusted. The truth is we may never understand why things turn out as they do. Even if we make mistakes, we need to be reminded that we have a loving God who sacrificed His only-begotten Son into death so that we might be forgiven. And forgiven we are: "Though your sins are like scarlet, they shall be as white as snow, though they are red as crimson, they shall be like wool" (Isaiah 1:18).

Perfectionism belongs to Jesus alone. We can rejoice that although we are not perfect, God has forgiven us through faith in Christ Jesus.

Notes: